A Pen's Music

A Collection of Poetry

By

Amy Childress

To my friend Cookie ...
for always
Amy Childress
Happy Birthday!
2010

PublishAmerica
Baltimore

First printing

PublishAmerica has allowed this work to remain exactly as the author intended, verbatim, without editorial input.

Hardcover 978-1-4512-0172-7
Softcover 978-1-4512-0193-2
PUBLISHED BY PUBLISHAMERICA, LLLP
www.publishamerica.com
Baltimore

Printed in the United States of America

Emily

I awake to the glow of the vibrant sun
I sleep as the moon circles the earth
Time so thin with fragile hue
Certain I am of the place in the end

Upon life's great shore I shall never take stride
Or ascend the mountain so high
But gracefully shall I live the world
As a blind man follows the sun

Evil Seeds

Willful wind
blow naive seeds toward the west
Plant them in the stomachs of foul girls
Who call themselves whores
Toward the salty sands of the dry heated lands
The rolling hills of California falling into the Pacific
The sun beating down against their dark hair;
Black sunset vanishes into the ocean as
lovers sell their souls for money
For lust, for love, for children
Using innocent men; harboring their children
Keeping their ships safe from rough water
Keeping their tiny seeds from being fed
Society wonders if they would be better off dead

Farewell to Summer

Farewell to summer and its
Languid purple haze
Treetops turn to red embers
becoming ashes on the sullen earth

In all of summer's glory
Lazy flowers bathe in the sunlight
Batting their eyelids against the warm rays
August's humid days glow like bronzed skin
Air floats above
A blanket covers the atmosphere
Keeping the warmth in

The tastes of summer simmer in the heat
Reds and yellows, greens and purples
a sea of nutrients

Soon frigid air will recall the sweltering heat
And freeze away the magic
Until the earth makes its round
And recalls its summer sounds

Clouds Through the Drive Thru Window

In the distance
The clouds converge to one vanishing point
As the sun sets,
the sky darkens
The orange glow disintegrates
And the purple shadows take over
Stealing the day

Center Aisle

She cannot walk
center aisle
Gown, pure as silk, hair fixed neatly
She cannot walk center aisle
Thirty years later, to do it over
To have his children
fix his meals
Wash his clothes
Make his bed
weekend after weekend
She is, a mother of pearls—
Wrapped tight into her oyster shell
Her sea of dreams eroding away
She cannot walk center aisle
Be a wife, a mother, a lover, a forgiver
Now fifty years, gone, without a trace
And she is alone

Again

Again I hope
Again I dream
Again I'm disheartened
With promises unseen
Again I cry
Again I ache
Again I lose
All for his sake
Again I'm tired
Again I'm confused
Again I follow
In my own mother's shoes

Secret Language in the Sky

They fly overhead
Speaking their secret language
As they caress the water's surface
I can't help but notice
The freedom they possess
And my craving for it

Candlelight

Candlelight flickers
revealing shadows upon the wall
but real is life's darkness
When night falls

A Couple of Opposites

She is a sponge
Porous, letting anything in that couldn't just as easily be squeezed back
out
He is a rock
Weathered and rough, pained with jagged edges
A tough skin that holds everything within

Cinquains

Societal Disorder
Don't eat
Society
Says not to; stay thin, frail
Be nonexistent, half living
Soul-less

Fake
Lifeless
Plant stares out of
The window—2 A.M.
Wishing to be alive and well
Outside

Inspired
inspired
Yellow walls ease
Black coffee is bitter
Both awaken the soul at best
And worst

Cocktails
Black dress
black heels and scarf
High, the room spins, a dream
Moonlight dancing in the rain mist
Alone

Black Space
He sings
Strums guitar and
Keeps time with the drummer
give me more, he says, inhaling
Black space

Blossom
Blossom
Sun filled petals
Arranged in a clear vase
Atop the grave of an unknown
Gray stone

Thinking
Silent
Except for life
Getting in the way of
All that is to be thought upon
Answer

Wings
Aloft
Soaring wings fly
Descending rapidly
Encountering resistance fast
landing

Waiting
Unless
A condition
Comes along and makes me
Fragile to stop and listen well
I go

Happy Yellow Field
Happy
glowing faces
Orange petals, long stems
Sunflower smiles beaming upward
heaven

Change
Loose coin
In my pocket
Or ever changing life
Never goes according to plan
Keep on

Mirror
Mirror
Of the sunshine
Reflections of the soul
If you look deep into the eyes
Of mine

Potential Energy

An empty vase
Contains no flowers
A dry tongue
Without words
A safe distance
Because closeness fails
Circle of energy derails
Potential
Not enough for what could be had
Stellar mind is quick to ignore
That which was paid attention to before
An effort without luster
Like dull rocks eroded over time
No hint of light on energy shines
Further into years and age appears
Across divided highways of time
Potential
Is lost

Adrift at Sea

Once whole
Components now adrift at sea
Busy men
Make me whole again
Rough waters
Carry a sailor's plea
Release the calm
And set us free

At the Party

Lit candles fight to stay alive against the cool evening breeze
tiki torches fluorescently glow
music dances inside everyone's ear
Filling them with rhythm
They bend like blades of grass in the wind
The light of the moon casts down upon them
Making their bodies shine
Their clothes wrap tight around their chests
They swig beer from cans
The men stare in delight
Inside, outside, upstairs and down
They move to the beat of their own drum
Smiles and laughter resound through darkness
illuminated faces glow
I sit alone behind the glass
I watch and I write this

Reasons

The wind is still for reasons unknown
God forgives for reasons unknown

Earth is silent, sphere in black space
We are intelligent, we think, for reasons unknown

Nature sings its song while the world is at war
A child is left to die for reasons unknown

Chorus of the storm; thunder drums, lightening sings and rain dances
We sleep at night and forget our dreams for reasons unknown

He breathes softly as he sleeps, tiny whispers of feathery air
And the harmony of life continues for reasons unknown

Deer in the Field

Remember when
We drove out to that field
And we saw the hundreds of deer
Gathering
Feasting
Oblivious to us as if no one was there
They carried on the way deer do
And we just watched
To see if our existence could be as peaceful as theirs
But it wasn't
That's why we watched
For the serenity of it all
Pretty soon they disappeared into the woods
A silent stampede of grace
We couldn't follow
So we turned around and went home
Taking it slow
Looking for more deer on the way
Hoping they'd find us
To fill the bond between us
And make life softer to walk upon

Where the Truth Lies

Sometimes I think its in his words The truth behind, the meaning implied, so far beyond what words can say Sometimes I think it lies within reality The intertwining of dark and light creating the hidden meaning of truth Sometimes I think its in his eyes When he doesn't whisper a single word But the feeling exists and is expressed in his gaze Sometimes I think its in his hands When his touch bears more significance than words ever could Sometimes it lies within his words yet it runs much deeper than that Where love and solemn truth reside with his heart, mine shall perpetually abide

The Moment

Why doesn't it last?
The sense, the feeling that once was
Never to be again
Invisible now to the time it once began
Escaping into the hard drive of our mind
Allowing itself to never resurface
Until touched in some way or form
That feeling, lost in a moment
Never regained
Almost forgotten…until…

Daddy
A
L
I

Your mind
A wasteland
Highs and lows
Create your masterpieces
The ones in your image
A part of you painted on canvas
Generations to come
Your tapestry is dark
The angry shadows that haunt you
Childhood reflections
Do these thoughts calm your senses
The edge is near
Courage soars sky high
In a glass bottle's lullaby

Sea

Inspired by wind and the energy of the sea
Its power over the greatest of man's genius
The workings of the tides plough upon the earth bearing no significance
To pound the sand they serve
Harborer and taker of lives
Beauty and possession house its mighty cavity of lifeless treasures
Casting shadows upon the living to be feared
An open grave to trespassers
A calm view to restless souls who dare to enter its waters
    Averse to its darkness and charmed by its sounds
    Engaged in its depth as it consumes all it surrounds

Ohio

Spiraling downward into his sea of blacks and blues
shades of his conscience weaving its way into my own
A masterpiece of charm and fantasy
I lie awake, hear his lungs fill with musty hotel air, I watch him exhale,
afraid to move, to disturb his slumber, afraid to allow my voice to be
heard, afraid of his own opinionated sword that often stabs and wounds
but sometimes makes me feel safe
On and off again his mind so quick to sparkle as a flickering flame, he
pulls me further into his web of passion, spidery threads lock me in,
wrap around my soul
He is merely a child sleeping soundly on our hotel bed, and I am afraid
to wake him, careful to intrude
He has me right where he wants me

Another Story

It could've been another story
The one that was meant
Instead of the one that happened
In another time, another place
What was invisible to us then, defines us now
The fateful knowledge that redirected our paths
Rising unnoticed, and always thus,
Always because, and only because of reasons unknown to us then
Moments so full, a heart not large enough to contain
It is you I know, and you who knows me
Without disguise my dreams reveal your honest eyes
And when this life is over, and we melt into memory and earth
What shall remain of us?
A whisper in the air beholding nature's favorite secret
Beyond us, time is only a measure of meanwhile and the future
As for the softness of the present, our time is now

Asches to Asches

Mein mutter is scattered amongst the Atlantic
Migrating home to her motherland
Riding upon unconquered waves
Rising above immeasurable swells
Diving into the coral
Occupied in the belly of a whale
She is Jonah, a hero
a memory fallen into asche
Pollinating the waters with her goodness
Goodenacht mutter
Sie grabstein warten auf
Free from the dangers of living
Once asked why we suffer
because we live
A warrior of water
The Atlantic, a temporary home before her next life begins

Symphony of Fear

There is a symphony of fear
An orchestrated pain
That lives within the walls of
Her domain
An anxious melody of soft piano keys
Living within the hardened tones
Of brass trumpets
And whiny saxophones
Abrasive trombones and shrill flutes
Her mind is alive but her heart is mute
A lonely cello groans
An octave lower than the rest
She plays with vigor anyway
to conquer life's quest

Ivory Keys

The ivory keys seem to calm him
Seem to put him at ease
Upbeat staccato
Soft mezzo piano
Highs and lows of
sounds that are soon invisible within the air
Beyond words
Lost inside of the notes he plays
The shrill voice with which he sings
He dampers the pedals
Restraining his thoughts behind the music
Releasing his emotions
Within the fluid sound
And it is only then, he lives

Two Drunken Philosophers

Two drunken philosophers
Stagger together 'neath the full moon
Their voices thick, language slurred with musky scent
Poison in their blood; no longer red
Color of life
What time is, they say, is incomprehensible
What life is, they question
What anything is, ceases to exist
Explain what life means and I'll tell you if you're wrong
Come my friend, together we question life, together we belong

Mysterious Woman

Mysterious woman, so close to me
Said I was special and could be anyone I wanted to be
Mysterious woman, why do you look so sad?
Have you not the life you've wished for me?
Mysterious woman, you worry me so
Bearing secrets from long ago
Mysterious woman, you've encouraged me to dream!
To live alone if marriage is not want it seems
Mysterious woman, you puzzle me so
Allowing your secrets to keep you from life
Mysterious woman you have not grown
Free from the choices and plans you have sown
Mysterious woman, what keeps you like a child?
All of your thoughts are restless and wild
Mysterious woman, what crosses do you bear?
To hold yourself back from all you've to share
Mysterious woman, you look tired and shamed
Lost in the world seeking answers from those you've blamed
Mysterious woman, so strong in your faith
Have you not the discipline to relieve your own fates?
Mysterious woman, I cannot watch you drown
So close within reach of a smile
Mysterious woman, why must you shed tears
Has pain kept you in bondage all these years?
Mysterious woman, you push me away
Not too close you always did say
    Mysterious woman, evaporate your feelings of old self worth
    And allow them to fall as rain down to earth
    Mysterious woman, reincarnate your desires
    Give birth to the new you and relinquish your fires

Minutes into Hours

As regulated as the minutes of everyday
The seconds that form the minutes that form the hours
The bustling world that never halts
For the mother who cannot afford bread for her child

The seconds that form the minutes that form the hours
Of the long nights that the insomniac suffers
Or for the mother who cannot afford bread for her child
Or the time wasted by young teenage girls wishing their life away

Of the long nights that the insomniac suffers
Time does not stop for the man who lost his wife
Or the time wasted by young teenage girls wishing their life away
Time continues on like a train; death its final station

Time does not stop for the man who lost his wife
For the insane who are trapped in their own minds
Time continues on like a train; death its final station
Time is finite; it will soon run out

Full Moon at the Beach

Evaporating fizzies in the hot tub at night
Jump from the bubbles
Like sitting on the edge of a soda glass

Marriage

Unintended for us to see
At the moment our very eyes met
What fate has for so long known
That our hearts become set
Upon the foundation of time
That has molded our lives
upon the threshold of love
lasting for all time…

Sacrifice

The café is dim
Filtered sunlight creeps through,
Illuminating her tiny hands
Reflecting off of her wedding band
So young when she said "I do"
Her dreams, delayed
Children played tired songs of life endlessly upon her heart
The creation of one meant having her own dreams depart
From her desire,
    Passion,
Her fire became rain, studded with nails and soured disdain
Her life, once free,
Now a mere breeze drifting further out to sea
Her children grew and etched their silhouettes
Residing inside a locket engraved upon her heart
Mother is beautiful behind the ceramic coffee cup from which she
slowly sips
The shadows creep in, the sun is setting
But not upon her dreams for her children

Smell of Sleep

The smell of sleep
At 6 am
The soured pillow
From nighttime dreams
His compass points North
Pinot Grigio burns going down
Like white acid
Smooth as silk
Dinner is soured
Soul music plays
Love once was, now in question
Gravity holds down the words we dare to speak
Like biting bitter fingernails
It is the life upon our own two hands
The life within our minds
The space of what we choose to fill
Resides with no directional signs

The Human Sky

You hear one, then two, then a thousand all at once
Silver teardrops fall
subside in the eyes of the tearless
anticipate a secret release
A violent storm within causing a catharsis of deadened emotion
Silver tears our sky weeps,
we weep
Recycled water that lies above and beneath us, within us,
Falling on us for generations
As our sky grows cold and
Sleepless, it darkens and growls
Yet after the rain, after the bitter taste of acidic tears have been released,
life continues on
Renewal of hope

Walking down the Street

I wondered what I looked like
To an outsider passing by
On a silent street
With no distractions except my smile
And my hair flying behind
I wondered how I seemed
To the world that doesn't know me

Suddenly I Realized

Suddenly I realized that the age lines on my face were symbolic of two crows perched on the outside of my eyes and my smile was wearing thin

Because these birds,

They do not fly away

Suddenly I realized that cellulite and varicose veins are roadmaps filling quickly with potholes on once flawless skin

the Department of Transportation is quick to ignore

Suddenly I realized my hair is more fragile and turns a grayish white— ugly within a dirty blond mane

Yes, Botox and hair dye, sure, they will cover up time's erosion

A new war is waged on time

These battles are a mere concealer for what is beneath

Suddenly I realized the dry spells…down there

No longer juicy times or sexy thrills—instead it is replaced by methodical, mechanical fake shrills

Suddenly I realized my loose skin—food clings

Fifty calories is one hundred calories

and the mind, the limits of the mind and its diminishing power over the years…

Suddenly I realized soy parfaits with vitamins would never replace my hunger for cheesecake and maintaining balance no longer applied to stepping on a scale but learning how to say no

Suddenly I realized I had to quit denial, to embrace age and conquer youth!

And forget its all happening??

Suddenly I realized fatigue sets in, a dark shadow that laughs at the very thought of becoming thin again

And energy is another word for sleep

Suddenly I realized my fire needed to be lit and my doors opened to the end…

Divided

At a crossroad
Divided
United as one
Divided by two
Can only take one way
Which to choose
Or do you turn back
Would you really lose?
Keep going, left or right
Quick make a decision
Or does fate make it for you?

Brilliant Light

Wattage
Brilliant light
You feel
Coal fired watts warm the children's cold home
Drafts and blankets
Green times are coming
Where will the watts come from daddy?
Winter comes again
Wattage
Brilliant light

So…About Sundays…

What if I don't go to church every Sunday?
Does that make me more of a sinner than I already am?
What if I don't wear polka dot dresses with stockings and high heels on
Sundays
Does that mean I'm less of a person,
    disrespectful in the eyes of God?

Judge not…
    Oh but you do!

I see through in my own faith…mine is not a hypocritical sort
    Like yours…

    Gossip on Sundays—yes…you
With the Gucci bag and Liz Taylor suit
Did you hear? Yes, her! Can you believe it? No, I never!

Have you though?
Ever thought differently
Reverently
Respectfully
At His creation
Outside of the box
Of your church?

On an Epitaph…

F**!!**#g dogs
        You just don't understand the physics of it!
Dammit!
        Life revolves around the dogs

    Some people should not have a driver's license

We've got idiots running this country

When I'm dead and gone, you can start over again.

Beds

We really should
Make the beds we lie in
Or, leave them in a tangled weave of a web
And be spiders that mate occasionally
Or we could just be ourselves
And tackle the hard mattress of our fears
Jumping in head first
Trying not to cover up our demons
Pink sheets soften our dreams
At night
dark colors make the world more vivid
comforters do not always provide comfort
night sweats more like it
but what for?
Water escaping from our pores
Soaking mattress
Wet dreams
But not the teenage kind
The scary kind, when your thoughts melt into your body and trickle out
like rain
Yes
We really should make the beds we lie in
Our dreams will have order

Different

They order two bloody marys
And sip them slow
The morning has arrived
To file away yesterday's pain
Of just being themselves
Dutiful nature
Has no rhyme or reason—it just is
Bellowing out its call
To those who hear
they bear shame
Stricken by sun's flame with golden hue
Masters of deceit until recently
Coming out
Challenging us all to accept
That which is different